GOP FRANKENSTEIN—
TEARING DOWN OUR GOVERNMENT.

1. Just When You Thought the 2016 Presidential Campaign Could Not Sink Any Lower

2. Trump and Breitbart's Stephan Bannon Choose the Nuclear Option

3. The Gathering Threat to Government from GOP Propaganda

4. The Connection Between Campaigning and Government Bashing

5. GOP Strategy to Smear its Opponents

6. The U.S. Supreme Court Empowers the Oligarchs

7. Who Gives Trump His Destructive Ideas?

8. Profile of Trump Supporters

9. Profile of a Model Republican

10. Mistakes and Lessons Learned

Foreword

Republican National Committee Chair Reince Priebus was ready to pull out his hair over conflicts between the Trump Campaign and Republican Leadership on Capitol Hill. House Speaker Paul Ryan refused to appear on the same stage with GOP nominee Donald Trump after Trump's 2005 rant on groping women surfaced.

In return, Trump branded Ryan as a disloyal and ineffective leader. Trump's alleged sexual exploits have Christian conservatives on edge. Vice Presidential

Candidate Mike Pence stepped back, unsure of what to do. Pence decided the Christian thing to do was to forgive the penitent. Trump, however, had no contrition in his heart, only fighting words that Bill Clinton did worse. Trump and his Campaign

CEO Stephen Bannon (former Breitbart News Executive) decided to go nuclear. It did not matter if Hillary Clinton had more qualifications than Trump to be president. Trump and Bannon would trot out so many accusers against Bill Clinton's alleged dalliances that enough Hillary supporters would stay home on November 8 (or so they thought).

How did the GOP create the Trump Frankenstein and abdicate leadership of the conservative movement to the nihilists and amateur revolutionaries supporting Trump? Republicans are more skilled than are Democrats at advertising, at selling soap, and in conducting Opposition Research. Of course, political campaigns are supposed to be sharply contested contrasts in selecting the "better" candidate.

The ultimate aim of Opposition Research, gone rogue, however, is to spread a smear that takes the opponent out of the race. Republicans always fear and smear the qualified opponent. George McGovern flew dozens of missions as bomber pilot in World War II. The GOP smear in 1972 was that he was weak on defense. John Kerry heroically captained a Swift Boat in Viet Nam.

The GOP solicited condemning affidavits from Viet Veterans to bring Kerry down in 2004. John O'Neil and Jerome Corsi, on cue, co-authored a book, *Unfit to Command,* Swift Boat Veterans Speak Out Against John

<u>Kerry</u>. However, Kerry did not respond to the jackals yapping at his heels. He was Swift Boated, a new term on the political lexicon.

George W. Bush had four more years to resolve the mess he caused in Iraq in 2003, but Bush could not put the genie back in the bottle. Republicans would blame President Obama and Hillary Clinton for the Iraq mess, the Syria mess, the Afghan mess, and the terrorist attack on the U.S. Mission at Benghazi, Libya, on 9/11/2012, and the death of four brave Americans.

Republicans smear Democrats, and at the same time call into question the foundation and legitimacy of the very government, which provides structure and protection for all Americans. Sharron Angle (R-NV) opposed Harry Reid (D-NV) for Senate in 2010. She lost by 41,424 votes, and claims Reid stole the election by voter fraud.

She suggested during the campaign that aggrieved Republicans resort to *"Second Amendment Remedies"*. Angle and other Republicans advocate measures to suppress the vote, knowing that a large voter turnout generally favors Democrats. Trump wants to take the country back to an era more favorable to GOP candidates, when blacks and other minorities were intimidated. Tea Party Republicans did not come to Washington to fine tune government. Tea Party dissidents wants to tear down government.

The GOP Freedom Caucus in the House wants to dismantle large departments of government. Stephen Bannon and Donald Trump want to bring down Paul Ryan. Trump joined the chorus that questions the legitimacy of government.

If Trump loses in Pennsylvania, he already blamed alleged voter fraud in Philadelphia. If he loses in the Electoral College, he has already said, *"The System is Rigged"*.

Republicans have created two monsters. Trump captured the Republican Party. He intends to remake it in his dark image. The Trump Effect in 2016 jeopardized GOP control of the U.S. Senate. If Hillary Clinton wins by more than ten points, the GOP may lose its dominant position in the U.S. House.

The other Republican monster is the disdain for government espoused by GOP leaders and policies over the past fifty years. Universal Healthcare with an individual mandate is a Republican idea that goes back to Richard Nixon. Barack Obama used as a model the Massachusetts Healthcare Plan that Republican Governor Mitt Romney signed into law in Boston in 2006. MIT Professor Jonathon Gruber counseled Romney and Obama on healthcare.

As soon as the Nation's first Black President embraced the GOP idea of universal healthcare, Republicans refused to touch it. **Not one** GOP member of the House or Senate voted in favor of the *Affordable Care Act of 2010* ("ACA"). In the last five years, GOP House Members voted more than fifty times to repeal, defund, or otherwise *cripple* the ACA.

Trump is leading a group of angry voters, many of whom want to stage a revolution if Trump is defeated on November 8. Alex Jones of Infowars.com, and Stephan Bannon and the Alt Right Gang at *Breitbart News and Views from the Dark Side,* are delighted with the chaos caused by the Trump Campaign. The troglodytes in the fever swamp and in the man caves are girding for battle.

Fifty years of GOP tearing down Americans' faith in the institutions of government is yielding a destructive result that should have been expected and avoided. GOP Leaders Paul Ryan and Mitch McConnell will suffer in January from chaos of their own making. Germany suffered takeover by an egotistical, intolerant, belligerent misogynist because its leaders failed to condemn obvious aberrant behavior *before* the tyrant could consolidate power.

As a *minority* party, the GOP should not allow a *minority* of its members to wrest control from the majority in a blatant attempt to do harm to the body politic. At the same time, the GOP undermines democracy by an organized effort to suppress the vote, intimidate minorities, and to maintain control by gerrymandering state and federal election districts.

Paul Ryan and Mitch McConnell are busy counting seats in Congress, apparently oblivious to the harm Republicans are inflicting on the Nation. GOP leaders evaluate Trump solely by the expected loss or gain of Congressional seats and control of State Government that will result from rejecting or endorsing Trump. GOP leaders seem indifferent to the risk of harm to the institutions of government resulting from conservative policies that defame and denigrate government.

Billionaires like the carbon king Coke Brothers have two missions for government. First, keep taxes low. Second, keep carbon regulation low to minimize economic burden on their fossil fuel empire. Charles and David Coke spent $10 million to save Governor Scott Walker (R-WI) from recall in 2012.

It may be just a coincidence, but Walker does not favor environmental protection regulation, state or federal. The U.S. Supreme Court eviscerated reasonable attempts by Congress to regulate campaign financing. *Citizens United v. Federal Election Commission*, 558 U.S. 310 (2010) equated money with speech that is protected by the First Amendment. *Citizens United* found unconstitutional campaign finance regulations embodied in the *McCain-Feingold Act* (*Bipartisan Campaign Reform Act of 2002*) (2 U.S.C. § 441b).

Our democracy, based on one person, one vote, is at risk of preemption by the oligarchy. Big Donor Money will displace the voice of the People. In the meantime, Donald Trump and Stephan Bannon are waging the most counterproductive, cringe worthy, cynical, dark, deceitful, destructive, un-American Campaign in U.S. history.

Chapter 1
Just When You Thought the 2016 Presidential Campaign Could Not Sink Any Lower.

"Let Trump be Trump." That is what former Trump Campaign Manager Corey Lewandowski recommended. Many Trump supporters agreed. None of them realized how dangerous it would be to unleash a wounded, cornered, desperate, egotistical, pathological liar, who was determined to dismantle the Republican Party and disrupt the American political system.

The American People finally would be able to take the measure of the man who would be president. Trump let it all hang out in 2005 on an *Access Hollywood* Bus Ride with Billy Bush. Trump bragged how he could get away with sexually assaulting women because he was a star on his televised *Apprentice* show. As soon as he met a beautiful woman, Trump boasted that he would just start kissing them. Trump confessed to groping and fondling women against their will.

Fortunately, for the preservation of the American way of life, his bragging about sexual assault recorded on audio and, upon emerging from the bus, on video tape that the *Washington Post* released to the public on Friday, October 7, 2016.

Trump's graphic description of his cavalier, sexual abuse of women hit like a bombshell. House Speaker Paul Ryan canceled a joint appearance with Trump scheduled Saturday, October 8. Vice Presidential Running Mate Mike Pence was mortified. GOP Members of the House and Senate, up for election November 8, wanted to denounce Trump, but feared a backlash from Trump's diehard supporters.

Senate races in seven states were close enough that a two percent net move by voters for or against Trump could be the margin of victory or loss. The U.S. House likely would remain in Republican control—unless Hillary Clinton won by more than ten percentage points. Melania Trump, Donald's third wife, released a statement saying that this is not the man I know. Trump dismissed his confession of how he violated women as mere *"locker room banter"*.

Trump, however, was not in a locker room when he described his game plan for making unwanted sexual advances on women. He was on a professional business trip in the Entertainment Business. Moreover, several athletes spontaneously repudiated Trump's suggestion that locker rooms are places where men brag about their sexual indiscretions.

Trump never apologized for his illicit conduct and demeaning attitude towards women. Trump floated a halfhearted, *"I apologize if anyone was offended"*. At midnight Friday, Trump released a video statement that was a declaration of war on Bill Clinton's indiscretions in the '80s and '90's and Hillary's alleged abuse of Bill's victim's. In short, the Trump Campaign adopted the nuclear option.

Chapter 2
Trump and Breitbart's Stephan Bannon
Choose the Nuclear Option.

The Trump Campaign went through many gyrations of leadership, but never escaped the baleful control of the candidate. Corey Lewandowski energized most of the primary campaign by letting *"Trump be Trump"*. Trump's family forced Cory out in a valiant attempt to have the campaign and the candidate pivot to issues calculated to winning a general election.

Paul Manafort took over for a few weeks, completed the primaries, but constricted the Donald's compulsion for *"Trump to be Trump"*. There was also the Russian Problem. Trump began to look like the *Manchurian Candidate*, who hypnotically adopted the Party Line of Vladimir Putin, President of the Russian Federation. Manafort previously represented Viktor Yanukovych, Putin's proxy President of

Ukraine from 2010 to 2014, when Ukrainian Patriots forced Viktor out in a revolution against Russian domination.

Inexplicably, Trump continually questioned the need for NATO, trivialized Russia's invasion of Eastern Ukraine, and its military takeover of Crimea.

Manafort may have wanted to avoid violating the *Foreign Agent Registration Act* ("FARA") (22 U.S.C. § 611 *et seq.*), which requires a filing with the Justice Department for U.S persons who represent a foreign principal within the U.S. Trump's advocacy of pro-Russian policies, Manafort's Ukraine experience, and his continuance as Campaign Manager, could raise FARA issues for Manafort and for Trump.

Trump installed Kellyanne Conway as Campaign Manager in an attempt to soften the Trump Brand with women. Trump gave in to his dark side in his final appointment. When Trump sends out his disruptive tweets, it is usually after he surfs the internet and digests the day's dark stories from Breitbart News and Info Wars.com. Trump retained Breitbart Executive Stephan Bannon as Campaign CEO. This meant that the *dark side* would dominate the Trump Campaign.

Trump's 2005 confession to Billy Bush on the Hollywood Access Bus Ride swamped Trump's Campaign. Instead of issuing a sincere apology and asking for forgiveness, Trump countered that the Clintons' sins were greater. The Second Debate was set for Sunday, October 9, at 9:00 PM. Trump and Bannon staged a weird press conference before the debate.

They paraded Juanita Broaddrick, Kathleen Willey, and Paula Jones, who allege that Bill Clinton either assaulted them or sexually harassed them. They brought in one victim, Kathy Shelton, who was raped by a criminal defendant when she was twelve years of age. The Clintons' offense was that Hillary's employer at the time assigned Hillary as an attorney to defend the rapist in court. Juanita Broaddrick alleges that Hillary threatened her to silence Juanita's accusation against Bill.

Rudy Giuliani reportedly managed the follow up of the ghastly press conference with the Debate Commission. Giuliani insisted that the four women sit in the Family Box of the Trump Family. Since the Families of the Clintons and the Trumps shake hands before taking their seats, this would have meant that Bill Clinton would have to shake hands or snub three of his accusers.

The Debate Commission saw through Giuliani's childish scheme, and admitted the accusers to seats outside the Family Boxes. Giuliani's blind and spastic advocacy of Trump for President has tarnished the Giuliani Brand. His fawning and apoplectic performance at the Republican Convention in Cleveland was grotesque. Giuliani complains of the Clintons' alleged pay to play conduct. Giuliani's fervid and raging advocacy on behalf of Trump seems to be the ultimate pay to play scheme.

The Paula Jones saga is a classic case of the damage a defendant can cause to self by digging in their heels and refusing to settle. Paula Jones was an employee of the State of Arkansas. Bill Clinton was Governor. Jones claimed that Bill Clinton sexually harassed her by propositioning her.

The claim likely could have settled for less than $50,000, including attorney's fees. Bill, however, could not admit to Hillary that he did it. Hillary could not admit to the public that her husband did it. The Jones' claim entangled in the investigation by Special Prosecutor Ken Starr into the failure of Madison Guaranty Trust Company in connection with the Whitewater Land Development, of which the Clintons were investors.

In the Jones' lawsuit, Bill Clinton denied under oath that he had a sexual relationship with White House Intern Monica Lewinski. Ken Starr submitted a Brief for Impeachment after he sniffed out Monica's stained Blue Dress.

The House of Representatives eagerly impeached Bill Clinton for obstructing a civil suit and for lying under oath, which offenses do not seem to qualify as the High Crimes and Misdemeanors specified in the Constitution for removal of a president. The Senate reluctantly heard the dreadful sex case, with Chief Justice Rehnquist presiding.

Clinton ultimately settled with Jones for $850,000, paid Jones' lawyers $90,000, and paid court cots of $1,202. The Senate failed to find Clinton guilty of any of the Offenses charged in the Impeachment, but the damage was done. Bill Clinton recovered to be one of the most popular presidents in U.S. history.

Republicans never recovered. Ken Starr never recovered. One of the three legs of the opposition stool to Hillary Clinton in 2016 is the GOP smear that Hillary is not fit to be president because of Bill's sexual dalliances and Hillary's alleged meanness towards Bill's accusers.

Chapter 3
The Gathering Threat to Government From GOP Propaganda.

Since the twentieth century, there has always been a dark side and, frankly, a *lunatic* fringe to the Republican Party. Robert W. Welch and the John Birch Society saw conspiracies everywhere. Welch thought that Dwight Eisenhower and his brother, Milton, were communist dupes. Senator Joseph McCarthy (R-WI) destroyed many lives to find very few communists lurking in the State Department or in the Army.

McCarthy and his counsel, Roy Cohn, were in the process of destroying one more life during the Army McCarthy Hearings. Army Counsel, Joseph N. Welch of the Boston Bar, finally dispatched McCarthy with, *"Have you no sense of decency?"*

When the Department of Justice sued Trump for housing discrimination, Trump retained Roy Cohn as Defense Counsel—ultimately, settled without admitting liability—and promised to comply with the *Fair Housing Act* in the future.

Barry Goldwater (R-AZ) was viewed as extreme in his day, but likely could not pass the Right Wing litmus test in the twenty first century. Republicans worship Reagan as the quintessential role model for conservatism. Ronald Reagan, however, would be deemed too accommodating to Democrats in today's *'take no prisoners' climate'*. While Barack Obama blithely waltzed with Michelle on Inauguration Day in 2009, Republican Congressional leaders met six blocks away to conspire to oppose all things Obama for the next four years. (It turned out to be eight years of disloyal opposition).

In a cynical misuse of power, the GOP decided to finesse the two terms of a duly elected president. Mitch

McConnell freely admitted in 2010 that his legislative mission was to deny President Obama a second term. Not one Republican in Congress voted in favor of the *Affordable Care Act* ("ACA"), which was a Republican idea since the days of Richard M. Nixon (R-CA & NY).

The House voted more than fifty times to repeal, defund, or otherwise cripple the ACA. It was a rite of passage for newly elected Republicans in 2012 and 2014 to sponsor yet another bill to make health care the plaything of the insurance companies. Before the ACA, insurance companies could and did deny coverage by noting that the disease was the result of a previous condition. Insurance, it seems, is only for healthy persons, if you believe the insurers.

Underlying GOP policy is the theme that government in and of itself is bad. This goes back to Thomas Jefferson c. 1800, who reportedly opined: *'That government is best which governs least.'* Jefferson eagerly abandoned his small government principles when he promptly took action to more than double the size of the United States by signing the *Louisiana Purchase* in 1803.

Republican candidates try to outperform one another in proposing reductions in the size and scope of government. In the debate to determine which Republican would oppose President Obama in 2012, Governor Rick Perry (R-TX) wanted to eliminate three Departments of Government: Commerce, Education, and (oops, I cannot remember).

The cumulative effect of GOP criticism of Government is that a large portion of the public has lost faith in government. Trump/Bannon fan the flames of apathy, cynicism, and revolt, by smearing everything that Hillary

Clinton accomplished in the last twenty five years. Congressional Republicans magnify the smear by holding endless investigations calculated to further erode confidence in Government. The House Committee on Government Operations and Reform investigates just about anything the Government does. Darryl Issa (R-CA) chaired from 2011-2015. The present Chair is Jason Chaffetz (R-UT). The purpose of the investigations is to embarrass President Obama and Hillary Clinton, and to ridicule Government.

The Freedom Caucus and the Tea Party undermined Speaker Boehner for cooperating with President Obama and the Democrats. Mark Meadows (R-NC) filed a Motion to Vacate the Chair in 2015, a challenge to the Speaker. Boehner ultimately resigned.

Jason Chaffetz (not exactly a bleeding heart liberal) kicked Meadows off the Government Oversight and Reform Committee. Meadows, the Freedom Caucus, and the Tea Party complain that Speaker Ryan is not doing enough to help elect Trump.

On 9/11/2012, terrorists attacked the U. S. Mission buildings in Benghazi, Libya, killing four brave Americans, including Ambassador Chris Stevens. Libya, of course, was in chaos following the upheavals of the Arab Spring. The revolt against Libyan strongman Muammar Gaddafi sparked in Benghazi.

The U.S. Mission had CIA buildings and State Department buildings that were not contiguous and were not protected by walls. Chris Stevens and the CIA wanted to be in Benghazi despite the danger because that is where the action was, including the danger from unregulated militias and insurgents.

Hillary Clinton was Secretary of State. It was vitally important for Republicans to smear Hillary Clinton because she likely would run for President in 2016, to succeed Barack Obama. The Republican pay to play crowd was spastic. Newt Gingrich, Chris Christie, and Rudy Giuliani were shut out from lucrative opportunities. They were outsiders after George W. Bush's disastrous eight years from 2001 to 2009.

Christie was Governor of New Jersey, and had his eyes on the White House. Gingrich, Christie, Giuliani and Congressional Republicans did not want to run against Hillary, who would be a formidable opponent. Benghazi was a convenient vehicle to smear Hillary. There were five or seven or nine hearings on Benghazi (depending on how the count is made), but none seemed to disqualify Hillary for the 2016 race for president.

Kevin McCarthy (R-CA), House Majority Leader, was hand picked by John Boehner to succeed as Speaker upon Boehner's resignation. McCarthy announced that the GOP established a Select Committee to Investigate Benghazi, this time under Trey Gowdy (R-SC), to bring down Hillary's poll numbers.

House GOP Conference Members punished McCarthy for daring to tell the truth, and elected Paul Ryan (R-WI) Speaker. Gowdy stretched the Investigation out to try to affect Hillary's chances in the 2016 Presidential Election. Hillary Clinton testified before Gowdy for a record eleven hours.

A few months later, Gowdy issued the Majority Report, which was a dud. Republicans chose Gowdy for his prowess as a State and Federal prosecutor. Gowdy announced that the hearing would be conducted as a trial. Hillary was supposed to be on trial, but it was the GOP that was found culpable in their smear politics.

When the Select Committee on Benghazi failed to bring Hillary down (although continual GOP smears did drive up Hillary's unfavorable numbers), Jason Chaffetz as Chair decided urgent action was needed to avoid facing Hillary in the November 8, 2016, election. Republicans desperately sought to bring down Hillary over her emails while Secretary of State.

Instead of informing Hillary officially from the start that she could not use a private server for emails, the State Department Inspector General *waited five years* and, ultimately, referred the matter to the Justice Department *after* Hillary left State.

As time for the FBI Report on Hillary's State Department emails drew near, Republicans were as giddy as kids on Christmas Eve. There was a possibility that a weakened Republican Field (and ultimately Donald J. Trump) would not have to run against Hillary, if the FBI recommended an Indictment. The GOP pay to play crowd, including Gingrich, Christie, and Giuliani were ecstatic.

Hillary might not be on the ballot after all. Christie would remain unscathed as Governor of New Jersey until January 2018, unless indicted for involvement in the scandal connected with the George Washington Bridge Lane Closure. After January 2018, Christie would need some pay to play opportunities—so he became Chair of the

Trump transition team until things began to look bad for Trump. Christie just seemed to melt into the background of the George Washington Bridge.

FBI Director James B. Comey announced that the FBI did not recommend prosecution of Hillary Clinton for misuse of emails while Secretary of State. Republicans gasped. There would be an election, and Hillary likely would beat Trump despite twenty five years of GOP Clinton bashing and smearing. Jason Chaffetz was devastated, and invited Comey to testify before the GOP workhorse, the House Committee for Government Operations and Reform.

Comey explained on camera that no reasonable prosecutor would take the case. Chaffetz, almost whining, pleaded: *"Can't you indict her for lying to Congress?"* Comey said he would need a referral. Chaffetz promised, *"You will have one in a few hours."* Chaffetz feared a fair election.

Chapter 4
The Connection Between Campaigning and Government Bashing

Hillary Clinton is running as a Democrat, supporting many of the policies advocated by President Barack Obama. Hillary has changed her mind on trade, and now opposes the Trans Pacific Partnership trade agreement (TPP). Trade agreements by their nature are supposed to tear down tariff walls and quotas.

As one of the highest wage manufacturers, however, the U.S. will be at a disadvantage in any trade agreement that does not contain provisions that allow the U.S. to equalize trade imbalances and competitive disadvantages with tariffs and quotas. Since NAFTA and CAFTA stressed removing tariffs and quotas, the U.S. succeeded mainly in drafting provisions to eliminate goods produced by prison labor and child labor, and in improving working conditions of workers throughout the world.

As admirable as these issues are, they do not make U.S. goods more competitive in the world market. U.S. free market principles militate against tariffs and quotas, without which the U.S. cannot compete with China, Viet Nam, India, or Bangladesh.

At all events, Hillary could distinguish her positions from those taken by President Obama, without attacking him. Hillary's presidency could be seen as complementary to Obama's, and in many respects an extension of Obama's term. Donald Trump posed as the Change Candidate. Why should the voters want a change? According to Trump, the Nation needs a change because everything is wrong from the economy from jobs to immigration to the wars in Iraq and Afghanistan, and to the humanitarian crisis in Syria.

Trump must argue that everything the U.S. government does is wrong, and that Trump somehow can magically fix it.

President Obama gets no credit for guiding the Nation through the worst economic collapse since the Great Depression, which ended only with the economic spurt caused by World War II. When Obama took office in January 2009, the Bush economy was bleeding more than 700,000 jobs each month.

About ten million jobs created during Obama's two terms in office. Obama gets no credit from Republicans for saving the U.S. auto industry. Republicans wanted to allow market forces to bankrupt U.S. auto manufacturing. After Obama saved the auto industry, Mitt Romney tried to take credit for the save.

Obama took Romney's advice, and modeled U. S. healthcare on Romney Care. Obama sponsored the *Affordable Care Act of 2010* ("ACA"), when Democrats controlled the Congress. Republicans turned on the ACA with a vengeance rarely seen in U.S. politics. The mantra of *repeal and replace* gradually faded to *repeal and displace*. Republicans sued to block ACA as unconstitutional.

The U.S. Supreme Court ruled that the ACA could not pass muster under the Commerce Clause, but was a valid exercise of government power as a tax on those who refused to participate. *National Federation of Independent Business* (and twenty seven states) v. *Sibelius*, 567 U.S. ____ (2012).

The Court beat back a challenge to federal subsidies in *King v. Burwell*, 576 U.S. ____ (2015). The Act expressly allowed subsidies for insurance purchased through a State Exchange, but did not specifically authorize subsidies through the federal Exchange. The Court ruled that the difference in language was an accident. Republicans were furious again.

When Trump's poll numbers sank, he began a scorched earth campaign that questioned the fairness of the media and the legitimacy of U.S. elections. Bannon and Alex Jones were delighted. They could use Trump's flameout to sell services on Breitbart News and Info Wars.com. The Trump Revolution will not be joined by even the majority of Trumps supporters. Even Ivanka is having doubts. Even Melania must have an exit strategy.

Chapter 5
GOP Strategy To Smear Its Opponents

If you are not with us, you are against us, said. George W. Bush. There is an all or nothing tendency in U.S. politics. When Ronald Reagan beat Jimmy Carter in 1980, Republicans branded Reagan as a hero and Carter as a dupe. It turns out that Reagan was flawed. After the Iranian Revolution in 1979, Iran turned against the U.S. When Carter allowed the Shah to come to America for medical treatment, the lid blew off. The Ayatollah encouraged Iranian student revolutionaries to storm the U.S. Embassy in Teheran.

Dozens of U.S. Diplomats were taken hostage. Carter's planned rescue aborted after two helicopters collided. Reagan did not want to see the hostages released. Bill Casey, later Reagan's CIA Chief, informed Iran of Reagan's wishes. Reagan beat Carter. Iran released the hostages during Reagan's inauguration Speech. Reagan delivered weapons to Iran in exchange for helping to beat Carter in the 1980 election.

Reagan went on to wage an illegal war in Central America during the Iran-Contra Affair. Oliver North traded arms to Iran, and used the proceeds to ransom hostages held by Hezbollah and pay for the illegal war against the Contras in Nicaragua. Reagan was operating a criminal enterprise in the United States.

After he left office, Reagan truthfully said, *"I do not remember."* He had Alzheimer's.

It is a travesty for Republicans to hold up Reagan as a hero and Carter as a weak president. To this day, Republicans continue to make odious comparisons at Carter's expense. Republicans like to say that Obama is a weak president *'just like Carter'*.

Jimmy Carter had more moral authority in his little finger than Reagan had in his entire presidency. CIA Director William J. Casey died on May 6, 1987, a few days before the extent of Reagan's criminal enterprise could be uncovered by Congress.

Bob Woodward claims that Casey admitted from the hospital bed the diversion of funds in the Iran-Contra Scandal in *Veil: The Secret Wars of the CIA 1981-1987*. Casey's wife, Sofia and Independent Counsel Lawrence Walsh dispute the Woodward's claim. Walsh stated that there is no documentary evidence that Casey new of the diversion.

There is also no documentary evidence that Casey requested Iran to hold the hostages to help Reagan beat Carter. Oliver North was convicted of accepting an illegal payment, obstructing a Congressional Investigation, and destruction of documents. The court suspended the confinement sentence and ordered North to do 1,200 hours of community service.

His conviction was overturned on appeal because evidence was used against him that was obtained through Congressional immunity. The Trial Court later dismissed all charges when independent evidence of crime was not available.

Chapter 6

The U.S. Supreme Court Empowers Oligarchs

John McCain is a Republican, but saw the danger from allowing unlimited money to flow into campaigns. Most Republicans want to allow unlimited money to reach political campaigns, especially their own campaign. Senate Whip and later Majority Leader, Mitch McConnell (R-KY), was plaintiff in *McConnell v. FEC*, 540 U.S. 93 (2003), which upheld the *McCain-Feingold Act* (Bipartisan Campaign Reform Act of 2002).

The Act regulated *soft money* contributions to political parties (not campaigns) used to register voters and increase voter participation in elections, and did not directly limit speech of campaigns. *Citizens United v. FEC*, 558 U.S. 310 (2010) found parts of the Act unconstitutional under the First Amendment.

The U.S. Supreme Court equated money with free speech. The result is that democracy yielded to oligarchy. The voice of the people will be overpowered by the voice of a few dozen millionaires and billionaires.

Chapter 7
Who Gives Trump His Destructive Ideas?

Ivanka Trump has a good eye for the optics of the Campaign. How does the public view the Trump Candidacy? Jared Kushner, her husband, can evaluate policies. They each thought that the Campaign went off the rails towards the end of the primaries. They were instrumental in forcing Corey Lewandowski out as Manager. They were looking for a pivot towards a General Election approach, which might add the 15% of voters needed to expand the GOP Base of Trump followers to an Electoral College Majority.

Little did Ivanka and Jared know that the Donald had already unleashed forces that would tear apart the Campaign. Paul Manafort and Stephen Bannon were advisors to the Trump Campaign. Manafort took over as Campaign Manager for a few weeks. Trump soon appointed Kellyanne Conway Manager and Stephen Bannon CEO. Bannon's elevation to CEO signaled the end of the Trump Campaign as a viable political force.

Bannon was Executive of *Breitbart News and Views from the Dark Side*. It seems that Bannon is Trump's guru. Trump sends out his prolific tweets at all hours, after Trump fires up by reading the internet feed of *Breitbart News and Views from the Dark Side*—sometimes augmented by conspiracy theories dredged up by the Drudge Report and Alex Jones of InfoWars.com. If one were to analyze the incredibly stupid and divisive statements made by Trump in this Campaign, most of them came from Breitbart or Drudge, or Alex Jones, or all three purveyors of conspiracy theories.

Trump does not admire John McCain, ostensibly because the Vietnamese captured McCain. Breitbart had McCain in its sights because McCain is part of the ruling establishment elite in Washington. Breitbart wants to take down the GOP Establishment, starting with McCain and Speaker Paul Ryan. Breitbart blames McCain for effectively sponsoring Amnesty because of McCain's support for Immigration Reform.

In Trump/Bannon world, McCain is an apostate because McCain collaborated with Ted Kennedy on

Immigration and with Russ Feingold on limiting Campaign Finance Contributions. Trump criticized Paul Ryan as an ineffective leader, following Ryan's cancelation of a joint appearance with Trump in Wisconsin.

Breitbart does not like immigrants or minorities. Breitbart and people like Carl Paladino, Co-Chair of Trump's New York Campaign in Buffalo, thought Trump should go after Kisr Khan, who spoke out at the Democratic Convention against Trump's Moslem Ban. Paladino also contends that President Obama is a secret Moslem, which is a smear on the President, on Moslems, and on the U.S. as a Nation.

"We Will Make Bill Clinton Into Bill Cosby."

The nasty side of the Trump Campaign has the fingerprints of a maladjusted fifteen year old adolescent all over it. The threat of shaming Hillary for Bill's sex dalliances came from Stephan Bannon. Trump embraced the nuclear strategy. Trump would try to intimidate Hillary by trotting out Bill's accusers, who also accuse Hillary of shaming them or trying to intimidate them.

Bannon's plan backfired. Nine women complained that Trump assaulted them sexually. Trump's blanket denial of sexual harassment, made at the Second Debate, spurred complaints against Trump by nine aggrieved victims in one week. Trump also cynically misused the four Clinton accusers at the Second Debate. Bannon's nuclear strategy failed. T rump promised to bring Obama's half brother and Pat Smith, mother of Benghazi victim Sean Smith, to the Third Debate. Hillary was not rattled.

Bannon and Trump may have to abandon the sex shaming. Hillary likely is immune to attacks against her husband (after 25 years), and the nuclear option served mainly to bring out an additional nine women to complain of the Donald's alleged sexual assaults. The ultimate aim of the juvenile delinquents in the Trump Campaign is to suppress the progressive vote.

If the 2016 Campaign is mired in muck, Trump/Bannon hope that the Clinton voters will be discouraged from taking the time to vote. Governor Rick Scott (R-FL) has a more direct approach. In populous counties, where Democrats outnumber Republicans, the Governor may try to limit the number of voting machines available, prolonging the time needed for progressives to vote.

This is in addition to Governor Scot's ambitious and unconstitutional preparation of lists of voters to be stricken from the voter rolls because they may be ex-convicts or progressive leaning Hispanics.

Trump is also a fan of *Infowars*.com, a website maintained by the radical talk show host, Alex Jones. Most of Trump's nationalist attacks on immigrants and minorities can be traced back to Alex Jones and Stephen Bannon.

The claptrap influence on Trump from Gingrich, Giuliani, and Christie is Pablum compared to the venom brewed by Alex Jones and Stephen Bannon. If the American people needed a clue as to how they should vote, it should be decisive that Trump takes the advice of Jones and Bannon.

Germany Indulged Xenophobia in the 1930s

Paul Ryan and Mitch McConnell bear a heavy responsibility for allowing Trump to get out of control. *The U.S. political system is supposed to be rigged against destructive candidates*. The race baiting by Trump is similar to that by Hitler used to fire up the German People in the 1930s.

There is a danger in the U.S. that Trump supporters will resort to Second Amendment Remedies, voter intimidation, and vote suppression, to allow Trump elected President. If Trump damages the American political system, Ryan and McConnell will be co-conspirators. Equally culpable are Pence, Giuliani, Christie, Gingrich, and the GOP Conference on Capitol Hill. The Trump portrait is complete for all to see. We are not talking only about a woman abuser. *Trump exhibits characteristics that might appeal to a Fascist.*

He is authoritarian, anti immigrant, anti foreigner, egotistical, and has followers who are white supremacists and nationalists.

If Paul Ryan cannot stand on a stage with Trump because of Trump's failings as a human being, Ryan must condemn Trump, his racist policies, and his candidacy. Ryan's first obligation is not to preserve a GOP majority in the House. Ryan's first duty is to preserve our democratic Republic for posterity. It is not every Congressperson for themselves, Mr. Ryan. It is for the Congress to act for America *before* Party.

The issue is not whether Trump sexually assaulted two women or twenty two women. The issue is whether Trump appeals to Fascists, racists, white supremacists, and nationalists. It is clear that Trump has no respect for women. It is also true that Trump has no respect for democratic process. He already signaled his excuse for losing.

If he loses, it will be because allegedly the *"system is rigged"*. Trump will sabotage our election system whether in office or out of office. The damage could be terminal if Trump is in office. Trump supporters have promised revolution if Trump loses the election.

Trump Tries to Change the Subject

The topic of mid-October was the Access Hollywood confession by Trump, augmented by the testimony of the first nine women of 2016 to accuse Trump of past sexual assaults. In a campaign directed by the equivalent of maladjusted adolescents, what strategy would they use to change the subject from Trump's indiscretions? Suggest a drug test for candidates! Brilliant idea concocted by maladjusted adolescents.

Here is how Trump presented the proposed drug test. According to Trump, Hillary was all fired up at the beginning of the Debates, but allegedly barely able to make it back to her van after the debate. Trump's solution. Have the candidates take a drug test to determine *"what Hillary is on"*. Trump volunteered to take his blood test. Howard Dean thought that maybe a mental test would be more appropriate for Trump.

If you do not see the logic of Trump's proposed drug test, you do not understand the mindset of maladjusted adolescents like Trump and his advisors, Stephan Bannon and Alex Jones. Everyone wondered why Trump was sniffing through the Debates. Some thought Trump may be on coke. To dispel any suspicion Trump suggested that Hillary was on something. The maladjusted adolescents thought Trump would be above suspicion if he recommended a drug test for both candidates.

Melania May Have Lied

Melania Trump gave the game away in her softball interview with Anderson Cooper on October 17. Melania confessed that she had *two boys* at home. Her 11 year old son, Barron, and her husband, Donald J. Trump. Since boys will be boys, we cannot expect grown up ideas from the Trump Campaign. Melania denied that there was an encounter on Fifth Avenue between her and the writer (Natasha Stoynoff), who claimed Trump molested her at Trump Tower just before a scheduled interview with Donald and Melania.

The writer was accompanied by her fiend during the chance encounter. The writer's friend remembers that Melania held her baby and was wearing heels. Trump and Bannon reasoned that if Melania denied the chance encounter months after the assault, the writer's groping claim would be disbelieved. The writer, however, informed her Journalism Professor soon after the time of Trump's unwanted adances. By lying about the chance encounter on Fifth Avenue, Melania gave further proof of Trump's molesting the writer (who was a guest at the wedding of Melania and Donald).

Ironically and stupidly, Trump had Melania send the writer and People Magazine a letter threatening a lawsuit for asserting that the encounter on Fifth Avenue occurred. Trump will never file the threatened lawsuit. The writer and People Magazine have ample proof of the encounter on Fifth Avenue and the sexual assault by Trump. Melania's lame caution, that accusations should be resolved in court with evidence, fails to recognize that witness testimony is evidence. By inducing Melania to lie about the encounter, Trump proved the assault accusation.

The other topic Trump used to try to change the subject is his continual whining that the election is rigged. As a fiercely competitive man, he cannot bear the thought of losing the election. Most polls show him in a downward spiral. To protect the anxious man, the maladjusted adolescent whines that the election is rigged. Marco Rubio disagreed. Florida has a Republican Governor.

There is no evidence that the sixty seven Florida Counties will not count votes fairly. Trump's subversion of the election system cuts to the core of American Democracy. It is criminal incitement to riot for Trump to tell his supporters that the media and the GOP establishment are stealing the election.

Drain the Swamp

Trump promises to drain the swamp in Washington. Trump has the right idea, but the *wrong* swamp. Someone should drain the *fever swamp* where Bannon, of *Breitbart News and Views from the Dark Side*, and Alex Jones, of InfoWars.com, breed their toxic, maladjusted adolescent schemes and conspiracy theories. Trump has spent nearly eighteen months firing up his base, which may be thirty percent of the electorate.

If a dozen ideas come out of the fever swamp, ten are calculated to turn off African Americans, Hispanics, Women, College Graduates, and Evangelicals. Jerry Falwell, Jr, Chancellor of Liberty University, appears wedded to Trump until the bitter end. Politics makes strange bedfellows.

Trump turns out to be an anachronism. If trump were born in 1900, he could have run in the 1950s as the last great hope of Caucasian peoples. In the twenty first century, there are simply not enough angry white men to elect a narcissistic, bigoted, nationalistic, groper, to the presidency.

Trump Debate Preparation

Hillary Clinton took the debates seriously, and prepare by reviewing the issues. Trump ignored the First Debate, and lost decisively. For the Second Debate, Trump trotted out Juanita Broaddrick, Kathleen Willey, and Paula Jones, who claimed Bill Clinton assaulted them. Trump also presented a victim who was raped at age twelve, and Hillary was appointed Defense Counsel for the rapist.

For the Third Debate, Trump threatened to fly in Obama's half brother from Kenya, and Pat Smith, mother of Sean Smith, one of the four brave Americans killed by terrorists during the raid on the U.S. Mission at Benghazi on 9/11/2012. Pat Smith, of course, claims that Hillary Clinton murdered her son. With Debate Preparation like this, how can Trump lose?

Chapter 8
Profile of Trump Supporters

Trump supporters are not necessarily laid off workers. Many are small business owners who make $70,000 or more a year. The rant against immigrants and loss of jobs is a byline. The main concern is government taxation and regulation, especially for businesses that have a carbon footprint. There may be a blue collar compartment somewhere on the Trump Campaign Train, but most of his support comes from small independent business owners.

Former Majority Leader Tom DeLay was the prototypical Republican before he entered politics. DeLay was an exterminator, who grew his own business. He was not keen on environmental protection or regulation of pesticides.

DeLay knew his business, knew what his customers wanted, and just wanted government to get off his back. Taxes were anathema. If DeLay wanted to work ten or more hours a day, why could Delay not keep most of his hard earned money.

Elected to Congress in the 1980s, DeLay worked with Newt Gingrich during the GOP takeover of the House in 1995. DeLay became one of the most powerful people in Congress, first as GOP Whip and then as Majority Leader. When Gingrich had to step down, and Bob Livingston had to withdraw over indiscretions, DeLay pushed the nomination of Dennis Hastert for Speaker.

Trump's presentation of himself as protector of the working man is a myth. Donald Trump markets a wide variety of products from shirts to scarves. All of Trump's products are manufactured overseas. President Trump will do little to bring back jobs to the Rust Belt. It's all talk.

Other Republicans were teachers, including former House Speaker Newt Gingrich and Dick Armey, who replaced Trump as Majority Leader. Gingrich formulated the famous *Contract With America*, which turned out to be a *Contract On America*.

At the end of the day, Republicans are paid by their patrons to reduce taxes on the upper one percent. To do this, they must cut government services to a bare minimum. That leaves precious little for social programs. Republicans can serve the industrialist Coke Brothers and Casino Magnate Sheldon Adelson, or they can the People. They cannot serve both.

Republicans cannot openly advocate for the interests of the one percent over the interests of the People. The trick is to stress opportunity. Medical Savings Accounts are a great tax saving, but only for the wealthy. Converting Medicare to a Voucher System sounds attractive until it is clear that the vouchers have less value than the Government Program in place.

Privatizing Social Security is brimming with entrepreneurial excitement until it is shown that the average worker has a great risk to lose their retirement nest egg in the stock market. Republicans favor the free market, where they can make a buck, sometimes a fast buck. Republicans will spend six hundred billion a year on national defense, but were willing to let the automobile industry fail.

Chapter 9
Profile of a Model Republican

The model Republican wants small government and low taxes. However, model Republicans would also like the government to take care of their aging parents and to provide medical care when needed. The government should not provide services to immigrants, or allow them to have driver's licenses. Blacks should keep a low profile, and stop scaring people.

Everyone should go to Church, and make a contribution to Jerry Falwell, Jr. Abortion should be banned. If a Republican lady needs to, she can always go to Canada or Mexico. Decent people do not talk about sex, certainly not the way Mr Trump has in the past.

One problem with the republican prescription is that it needs an underclass for the Nation to work in an optimal manner. The modern Republican Party flourished on keeping blacks and immigrants in their place. Slavery was abolished in 1865 by the Thirteenth Amendment.

The Fourteenth Amendment (1868) conferred citizenship to everyone born in the U.S. and subject to it laws. The Fifteenth Amendment (1870) prohibited denial of the right to vote based on race,m color, or previous condition of servitude. The Civil Rights laws, now classified at 42 USC § 1981, et sq., are based on Civil Rights legislation passed in the 1870s. The Nation was serious about Civil Rights in the early 1870s. Blacks could and did run for, and were elected to, Congress.

It all fell apart after the election of 1876, where there was a standoff between Rutherford B Hayes (R-OH) and Samuel J. Tilden (D-NY). In 1877, the Compromise with the devil was that Hayes would pull federal troop out of South Carolina and Louisiana. Outgoing president Ulysses S. Grant pulled troops out of Florida. Reconstruction was over. Jim Crow was in. Hayes won the White House, the Democrats won the South.

Civil Rights would go to sleep for nearly ninety years. No more blacks would be elected to Congress until after the passage of the Civil Rights Act of 1964 and the Voting Rights Act of 1965. "Conservative" Democrats fled to the waiting arms of the Republican Party.

The stampede of Southern Democrats to the GOP was foreshadowed by the walkout of Strom Thurmond from the Democratic Convention in 1948 as a protest over a Civil Rights Plank in the Party Platform. The South was to become the solid South for the GOP.

In essence, today's Republican Party has no valid reason to exist. The Party was founded on principles in 1854 to celebrate free soil, workers' rights, and the rights of farmers and small businesses.

Chapter 10
Mistakes and Lessons Learned

It was a fundamental mistake for Hillary Clinton to base her 2016 campaign for the presidency on the theory that her opponent was not temperamentally fit to be president. If the assertion were true, all the more reason not to say it. The campaign would have been less toxic if Hillary would have presented the voters with her vision for America. Once one candidate threw the gauntlet on fitness down, the campaign was personalized on a destructive level.

It is for the voters to decide who is fit to be president. The person accused of unfitness is hurt to the core, and can be expected to lash out.

The level of animosity at the three debates was screaming for redress. To save his ego at the Second Debate, Trump presented Juanita Broaddrick, Kathleen Willey, and Paula Jones as accusers of Bill Clinton. The fourth guest was raped at age twelve, and Hillary was appointed defense counsel for the rapist.

Pat Smith, mother of Sean Smith, who died in the terrorist raid on the U.S. Mission at Benghazi, Libya, spoke at the Republican Convention, and accused Hillary of murdering her son. The 2016 Campaign was caustic, cold, surreal, and dark. It may have gone better if Hillary had argued on policy differences instead of character. Trump invited Obama's half brother to the Third Debate, which likely did not phase Hillary. The rumor was that Trump also invited Pat Smith and a fiancée of Sean Smith. Hillary was not rattled.

Trump's problem, and the Nation's problem, was that Trump viewed everything through Trumpcentric lenses. It was all about Trump. He had developed a brand over the years. His building bore the Trump name. Dozens of other buildings bore the Trump name because he licensed his name to third parties. Trump was incapable of analyzing an issue without first determining how the issue affected the Trump Brand and his fragile ego.

President Trump would be like having Walt Disney in the White House. Walt would be thinking mainly about Disney Land and Disney World instead of issues that affected other Americans.

The voters have a distinct impression of the candidates. Twenty eight million will vote for Trump. Thirty three Million will vote for Hillary. Trump claimed on many occasions that the election is rigged. He refused to accept the results of the election during the Third Debate. Some Trump supporters are ready for revolution.

It is important for Trump to concede defeat, if he loses. If Trump complains after the vote tally that the election was stolen, he may spark riots. If so, he will brand himself as a

Fascist, a strongman (but weak person) who does not believe in Democracy.

Trump began and ended his campaign with epithets. He dispatched Jeb Bush with *'Low Energy'*, and complained of *'Lying Ted Cruz'*. The rhetoric degraded from *"Crooked Hillary"* to *"She is such a nasty woman"*. Hopefully, Trump will stop campaigning and stop sniping on November 8, 2016.

Jason Chaffetz (R-UT) should make his New Year's Resolution for 2017 that he will not continue to investigate Hillary Clinton to obstruct government. If the Republicans continue to abuse their office with partisan politics, the voters will whittle away the GOP majorities in Congress and in the thirty states where Republicans dominate. Eight years of trying to delegitimize the presidency of Barack Obama served mainly to delegitimize the Republican Party as a viable political force.

If Republicans do not like the provisions in the *Affordable Care Act*, then join with Democrats and the White House to revise the Act so that it works for the American people.